Dedication

This book is dedicated
to all those who wake up one morning
and suddenly find that their head is damaged
and to those of the medical services
who help to alleviate that damage

I am very grateful to the many friends
- far too many to name individually -
who have supported me while scribbling
these varied lines
and without whose encouragement
none of these verses would ever
have seen the light of day

RICHARD HARTLEY

Acknowledgement

The quotation from *The Daily Telegraph* used in
the introduction, appears by kind permission of
Telegraph Media Group Limited

+ + + +

Introduction

I came late to poetry. At school, during English lessons, when we were set an essay to write, I was quickly bored so would do my own thing. Sometimes I would write a poem or sometimes a little play. Of course, they were rubbish and as I was completely without talent they were quite rightly forgotten.

Meanwhile, I often felt an urge or a calling to express myself but over the years I found no creative outlet for that expression. I sometimes thought about writing - either prose or poetry – but had a fear of ending up with poems where the rhyme was forced and the verse unreadable.

Some time around the turn of the century, I started listening to a late-night programme on the radio called *Poetry Please*, which was introduced by Roger McGough. I noticed that, more often than not, the poems did not rhyme but they did have a rhythm and a pace and there was frequently a cadence to the voice that made the words sing. Unknown to me at the time, a seed was planted in my mind which was left to germinate at its own pace.

Towards the end of 2015 I became ill and was diagnosed with temporal lobe epilepsy, meaning that my working life had to come to an end. Despite a few scares over the following weeks and months, never quite sure whether I was going to make it to the next Christmas, I have survived – thanks in no small part to the support of some kind friends and neighbours.

In 2016, Terence Davies released his film *A Quiet Passion*, about the American poet Emily Dickinson. At one moment during that film, Emily Dickinson is conducting an argument by correspondence with a newspaper editor who is publishing some of her poems: much to her annoyance, he is altering the punctuation of her poems and she asks him not to do so. Emily says [I paraphrase]: *"I put the punctuation there for a reason and if I have used a comma then I want you to use a comma too."*

Another little spark lit up in my head. Now I had rhythm and pace, cadence and punctuation, with no need to force the words to rhyme. It was as if I was suddenly given permission to put some words on paper and see what I could make of them. So that is what I did.

Then along came the third leg of the stool. The important leg. The leg that ensures no matter what the surface, the stool will remain standing despite resting on uneven ground. In July 2016 the obituary of Sir Geoffrey Hill appeared in The Daily Telegraph. The first sentence of that obituary read *"Sir Geoffrey Hill, who has died aged 84, was a poet and scholar whose combative and often impenetrable work led critics to hail him as one of Britain's greatest writers."* Immediately I thought to myself that if this man could write combative and often impenetrable work, get a knighthood for it and be considered as one of Britain's greatest writers, then maybe I could scribble away and at least produce something readable.

Shortly afterwards I was introduced to *Poetree Walks,* a local group organised and arranged by Gerry Donlon. This irregular group meet during the summer in the area of north Essex and Suffolk, on a weekend afternoon and walk through interesting woodland, pausing now and again to recite poems to each other while enjoying the natural beauty of the woods around them. I felt at home, both with the people and with the peace of the surroundings, suddenly feeling that I had everything in place to try and make the best of my scribbling.

This book is the result – and I hope you enjoy reading my poems as much as I have enjoyed writing them.

Mistley, Essex, England
July 2019

Index of Titles

+ + + +

An Early Spring Day

Standing on The Walls
Looking out across the river
To Suffolk on the northern shore.

The sky is clear
And deepest blue
With not a wisp of cloud in sight.

A hint of warmth
Invades the tranquil air
And sets in place a subtle haze.

No wind disturbs
This perfect scene
Or worries leaves on nearby trees.

The water, still
And smooth like glass
Lies flat across the estuary.

The seasons turn
And oh, what joy!
Spring is back with us once more.

+ + +

Me And My Bird

I am alone in my lovely sitting room.
Or at least, when I say I'm alone I'm not really alone
In my sitting room.
Because I am not alone!
I am sharing my room with a bird.

Not an attractive female who may have been invited
To share some quality time with me.
But a real bird.
A feathered bird.

Which may be a female but then maybe it isn't.
It might be a pigeon but it may be a rook.
Or even a crow
I don't know because I can't see it.
Because it's in the chimney.

And any moment now it'll be in my sitting room -
Covered in soot.
And spreading it around my sitting room.
As it looks for a way out.
And as I look for a way of getting it out.

Why is it in my chimney?
Because there's no wire at the top of my chimney.
That would have cost money.
And there's never enough money for the little things.
So when birds land on the top of my chimney,
Some lose their step.

And stumble.
And fall down the chimney.
And can't get out again.
At least, not the way they came -
Down the chimney.

But possibly out into the sitting room.
If they can find the gap -
Between the edge of the fireplace
And the wooden sheet
That's supposed to block it.

But it may not find the gap.
In which case it'll stay there
Getting weaker and weaker
And then it'll expire.
Which will be the end of the bird.

But it won't be the end of the bird.
Because it'll rot.
And then start to stink
And I'll have to open up the wooden sheet
To get the dead bird out.
But at least it won't spread the soot
Around my lovely sitting room.

+ + +

Eight Lines On A Piece Of Rock

Eight lines carved on a piece of rock
Not by nature but by man.
Cut deep and straight with love and care
Engraved in to this sacred slab.

Meaning lost from ancient time
Some deep thought or vague idea
Turned this stone to a work of art
That speaks to me from ages past.

+ + +

The Rook

When I saw the rook
On the inside
Of the window
I knew that she had died.

I rang the bell.
No reply.

Knocked on the door.
No reply.

Called through the letterbox.
Still.
No reply.

And the rook kept tapping
At the window.
From the inside.
Trying to get out.

I rang her phone.
No reply.

Got her key
And tried the door.
The lock turned.
But the door was bolted.
On the inside.

And still the rook pecked
At the inside of the window.
Trying to get out.

I know the house
There's no way in
For a rook.
When all the windows
Are closed.
Which they were.

My neighbour was small
And wiry.
Of ancient Welsh stock.
Proud and independent.

Aged ninety three
A widow now.
She kept her loss
And her loneliness
To herself.

The police were called
And when they came
They saw the bolted door.
And the rook.
Inside the window.
Pecking.
Still trying to get out.

A domestic bolt is no match
For a policeman's heavy boot
And it gave way
To one good kick.

Both policemen went inside
And into the room.
Where the rook
Pecked
At the window.
Trying to get out.

One policeman came outside
And showing tact
- As they did throughout the evening
Said
Yes
I'm sorry to tell you
That she's passed away.

And the bird?
I asked.

Ah, the bird
He said.
I looked at the bird.
It looked at me
Straight in the eye.
Then it flew
Out of the door.

The air was warm.
The evening still
And calm.
Beautiful and clear.

That's good
I said to my neighbour.
Yes
She said.
That's Olwen's spirit.
Flying free.
Off to join her husband
Who had died last year.

+ + +

Mistley Cricket Club

Sitting.
Looking out.
Across the field of play.

A cold pint of beer
In my hand.
At peace with the world.

The sun breaks out.
The clouds skit
Like chariots
Across the azure sky.

Cars murmur
On the nearby road
As they pass by
Beyond the hedge.

The church
Straight ahead
Holds the eye.
With tree-framed spire
Reaching up
To scrape the sky
And dominate the field of view
North towards the river.

Ringers toll the changes
And the bells peel out.
As they have
For many years gone by.

Michael wanders up.
We have a chat.
"Isn't this glorious"
I say.
"So English
And so wonderful"

"Yes"
He says.
"I have the word.
It's quintessentially
English".

Some may call it cliché
But all is there to see.
The field of play
Framed by trees
In every shade of green.

The hedgerow
- Neatly trimmed –
Nature's border
Beyond the rope
The boundary line

Where the laws of the game
Say the batsman
Will earn his four runs.

The over ends.
The umpires change.
One from stumps to now
Square leg.
The other vice to versa.

The batsman
Takes his stance.
The fielders tense
And walk
Their few paces
In towards the square.

The game goes on.
The view unchanged
From many years of play
At this
Most glorious of grounds.

+ + +

Fishing For Poets

I go to the poetry group
To listen to other poets
And sometimes read my own.
But she reeled me in!
She caught me like a fish upon a line
And reeled me in!

All I said was "I like your poem".
"Are you an actor?" she asked in reply
"Are you a film star?"
All I wanted was a chat
And possibly some friendship.
Nothing more.

Just as every time a fish
Opens its mouth
It fastens more securely on the hook.
So at everything I said or did
She pulled a little on the line
And reeled me in.

And just as, for a fish once caught,
There is no escape, so it was for me.
Soon the line was pulling tight
And I was dancing like a silver fish
Upon the crystal waters
Of a Downland chalk stream.

When all I wanted was a friendly chat.

+ + +

Bulbarrow Hill

I long to stand on Bulbarrow Hill
Once more before I die
And feel the wind upon my face
And blowing through my hair.

Looking west for forty miles
Across the Blackmore Vale
Or south towards the Dorset Gap
The land spread out below.

A tapestry of fields and woods
Seen from up on high
For sixty years I've known this view
And kept it in my mind.

If I don't go to Bulbarrow
Once more before I die
I know that view will go with me
And help to ease my mind.

+ + +

Ode To A Young Man

You were young
And in your prime
Good looking, well-travelled
And quite a catch.
- If you would be caught.

Playing with any team
As the spirit took you
Not a fixture in any group
But happy to float along.
– Just a free spirit.

With an open mind
And an open heart
Always open to new ideas
You had to try everything.
– At least the once.

Drifting through life
Without an anchor
Your open mind might
Cast you on the rocks.
– Or take you out to sea.

But the doors did not open
The way was not clear.
The currents pulled you
This way and that.
– So you just kept drifting.

+ + +

Aberfan. 21st October 1966

Shortly after eight o'clock
On that damp October day
A thirteen year old boy
Made his way to school.
In Swanage, on the Dorset coast.

The last before the half term break
This was to be a special day:
To mark our Foundation
And offer up our thanks.
Prizes in the morning
Then a hurried lunch -
Before walking through the town
For a service of thanksgiving,
In the parish church.

At last the Vicar took his place.
Standing to address the school
He called in his deep voice
For prayers - for the school children of Wales.

But we did not know -
That shortly after eight
On that damp October day
One hundred and forty children
Made their way
To just another primary school
At Aberfan, in the Welsh valleys,
130 miles away.

Not yet fully light on this dank and dreary day
It had rained for many days and still it fell.
The water ran down roads and filled the drains.
And, where it fell upon the hills, it soaked the ground
With murder in its heart.

The last day of school
Before the half-term break
No Foundation Day to celebrate
No thanks to offer up.
No prizes in the morning
Just the calling-card of death.

Shortly before nine the rain began to clear
And at the mountain tops blue skies appeared
To tease and mock the view.
But in the valley mist and cloud
Lay heavy in the morning air
Cutting sight to 50 yards or less.

Spoil Tip Number 7 was high up in the hills.
A mound of waste and stone and dust
Loose rock and mining spill:
Built up over fifty years
By the heavy hand of man
And corporate lack of care.

Water did what water does:
It made its way downhill.
And every drop of water took
Some speck of dust or rock
And grain by grain it ate away
To undermine that tip.

At 9.13 it made its move.
2 million tonnes began to slide
Down the hillside to the town below.
And as it moved it roared: a cruel rasp of death
Like a crashing plane they later said -
But all the while unseen by those below
Still shrouded in the morning mist
That blanketed the town.

Many thousand tons were scattered
On the hillside as it fell.
But not enough.
A quarter million tonnes
Hurtled on down
Wiping out a farm and 20 houses.

Before slamming into Pantglas School
At 9.15 A.M.

116 children and 28 adults too
Shared a brutal, early-morning death.
No prizes in the morning.
No prayers for their Foundation.
They didn't go to church that afternoon.
Nor start their half-term break.

Instead they lie in hallowed ground
At peace and free from harm.
They aged no more from that day on
But their names will live for evermore
Dear to those that loved them.

+ + +

Walk With Me

Take my hand and walk with me
Let me tell you about your life
I'll show you the Valley of Loneliness
And I'll try to tell you why.

We'll climb the ridge named Hindsight
And look down on the valley floor
For on that ground is laid a map
Of your life from birth till now.

Together we will walk that land
And I'll listen to what you say
As you tell me about the life you've led
And the feelings that you've had.

And in my turn I'll tell you how
That life has shaped your mind
And left its mark upon your soul
And made you who you are.

Memorial Day In Moscow

The lump of rock glistens in the damp, cold city
Set on a raised plinth in Lubyanka Square.
Its very presence mocks the infamous building opposite
Shouting defiant curses at those who once ruled this land.

Kokarev, Alexander Danilovich, 30 years old.
Expelled from the communal farm for being a kulak.
Shot. January 31st 1938.

The small knot of people starts to form and builds
By ones and twos from well before the dawn.
As the veil of night is slowly cast aside
The numbers grow, each year greater than the last.

Kokkinaky, Grigory Georgiyevich, 50 years old.
Member of the council of defence attorneys.
Shot. March 8th 1938.

This is not some grand imperious military parade
With men and machines following painted tracks
Along a broad and shuttered Moscow street.
Rather a humble, simple ceremony of quiet dignity.

Kazantsev, Yakob Yegorovich, 33 years old.
A father.
Shot. June 22nd 1938.

For now it is ordinary, everyday, decent folk
Paying their respects to honour the memory
Of victims killed in the dark forbidding past
Long dead - but not forgotten.

Jiganin, Ivan Georgievich, 59 years old.
Roads and waterways employer.
Shot. December 31st 1937.

While waiting their turn to perform their sacred role
On this open and exposed public stage
Each is handed a candle and a slip of paper
Bearing the name of one who is not here.

> *Eromenko, Grigori Mitrofanovich, 22 years old.*
> *Worker.*
> *Shot. March 16th 1938.*

Moving to the microphone they each in turn
Read out that written name and honour the memory
Of some poor citizen who didn't have a choice -
Who had no chance to argue or to plead.

> *Gerassimov, Nikolai Grigorievich, 33 years old.*
> *PE teacher.*
> *Shot. April 13th 1937.*

Each year those deaths sink further in the past
Yet each year more people come to play their part.
But so vast are the numbers to be remembered and recalled
It will be many decades before all their names are spoken.

> *Andrei Sergeevich, born in 1888.*
> *Participant of the First Russian Revolution.*
> *Four years hard labour from Tsar Nicholas.*
> *Executed by firing squad. July 1938.*

Fifty million human souls were killed
To satisfy the sick, barbaric plans
Of a simple Georgian peasant named Joseph Dzhugashvili
  - Known to the world as Stalin.

+ + +

The Last Train

Standing at life's railway station
Waiting for my train.
Many pass but they're not going
Where I want to go.

Escaping from the storms of life
I shelter in the waiting room.
And while I linger, killing time
Trains keep passing through.

Late at night the last train stops
But none get on or off.
I climb aboard with heavy heart
Not knowing where it goes.

This train will not be going
Where I want to go
But on and to the terminus
With a seat reserved for me.

+ + +

A Little Bit o' Rappin'

10 o'clock
11 o'clock
12 o'clock
Rap!

1 o'clock
2 o'clock
3 o'clock
Rap!

4 o'clock
5 o'clock
6 o'clock
Rap!

I'm rappin' all round the day!

Rappin' in the mornin'
Rappin' after noon
Rappin' in the evenin' too.

I spend my whole day rappin'
Rappin' just for you!

Rap! Rap!
Rap – Rap!
Rap!
That's all I ever do -

Ever since I got this crummy job
Wrapping gifts for you!

+ + +

A tribute to mark the 100th anniversary
of the first day of the Battle of The Somme, 1st July 1916

The Somme

My Great Uncle sailed to France.
As many Great Uncles did.
Along with many fathers
Brothers
Lovers
Sons and husbands.
To war
Across the channel.

It was fun to start with:
A great adventure.
An outing.
A picnic.
I know because I have his pocket book.

He wrote it up each day
From when he left England
To a sudden stop
When he died.
Along with many others.

In battles across northern France they fell.
The cream of our youth.
Battles honoured
In the telling
Of some obscure village name.
But the worst of all to English ears
Was The Somme.

The Somme.
With greatest casualties
Suffered by our army
On a single day.
Ever.

Start of battle first July.
Crack of dawn.
It was "Line up boys and over we go".
After the artillery was supposed to clear the way.

Some commanders knew
The nature
Of the war they fought.
But they were over-ruled.

"Listen to what I'm saying, young man"
Haig told a subordinate.
"I am giving you the benefit
Of my experience".

But his experience was irrelevant
And the subordinates listened too much.

Far too much.
And many died.
Far too many.

Over the top –
A hail of bullets.

Through our wire –
A hail of bullets.

No-man's land
At walking pace –
Another hail
Of bullets.

Closer now but fewer left –
Another hail of bullets.

Not so many now to face them –
But yet another
Hail of bullets.

Bodies left just where they fell.
But many less are walking now.
Facing
Yet another hail
Of bullets.

Most of them they died
That day.
Shot
Mutilated
Drowned
Or gassed
19,000 in a single day.

Nine. Teen. Thousand.
In.
One.
Single.
Day.

One single day
That didn't always get
A single yard
Of muddy soil.

That battle
Lasted to November.
Carnage upon carnage.
Day after day.

But it started on
Saturday
The first of July
Nineteen Sixteen
When 19,000 men died.
At The Somme.

+ + +

The Rose

With colour deepest yellow
Petals soft as silk
It reaches up and draws me in
As I was drawn to you.

Gently lifting up the bud
To just below my nose
I smell your sweet delicious scent
That scent I knew so well.

Lifting up the rose again
To stroke across my eyes
I feel the softest touch of you
That touch I knew so well.

Raising up the rose once more
To brush against my lips
I feel the sweetness of your kiss
That kiss I knew so well.

That scent, that touch, that kiss of you
I knew them all so well.
This rose brings them back to me
From forty years ago.

+ + +

A Younger Tree

It was nearly six
And time
To wind down for the day.
Time for a drink
To start
The evening's tumble into night.

From my window I see Tony
Sitting on the bench
Outside his house.
Reading.

I wander over
And ask him:
Are you enjoying a peaceful moment?
Or would you welcome company?

We have a chat
And then agree
A glass of chilled white wine
Would be perfect right now.

I nip into my house
To my well stocked fridge.
And return
With two glasses
Of *pinot grigio*.

We sit and talk.
Admiring
The view laid out before us.
Every Pantone shade of green
Set out like a colour chart
In the trees that we can see.

Trees and trees and yet more trees.
Straight ahead
To left and right.

There are three decaying oaks.
But these noble trees
Seem most reluctant
To leave the stage.

Sending out a last defiant burst
Of brilliant green in clumps of foliage
Making more stark
The grey skeletal frame
Of the dying tree.

There's a perfect curve
Where -
Quite by nature's chance
Three trees are canopied together.
And combined
Produce a stark green border
As sharp as any draughtsman's line
Against the bright blue background sky.

Over to the right
A younger tree.
Smaller.
Straight of trunk.
With leaves of bright, yellowy green.

From that tree
Looking back
It sees across the village green
My house in Suffolk Pink.
The oldest within view.

That tree will be my resting place
When my time on earth is done.
It's where my ashes will be thrown.
So I can always look
Back across this perfect scene
To the house
Where late in life I found some peace.

+ + +

The Estuary

Sitting at the river's edge
With Mistley at my back
Looking out across the estuary
To Suffolk - on the other side.

The sky a deep and cobalt blue
The air so still and calm
Not a breeze to stir the leaves
Of the trees lined up behind me.

The summer tide is in and high
The water clear and flat
Stretching - like a pane of glass -
Towards the northern shore.

Up beyond that shore are spread
The colours sharp and clear:
The cornfields - dry and dusty-drab
Form a backdrop to the view.

Woods and trees and hedgerows too
In every pastel shade of green
March across the countryside
Firm fixtures on the gentle land.

Parked like toys upon the river
Boats tied to their moorings
Lie peacefully - upon the flat
Still, surface of the water.

A line of swans sails in to view.
Gliding smoothly and serene
Their strong, firm paddles underneath
Drive them east - towards the Quay.

Traffic passes on the road behind.
But even that intrusion cannot blight
The peaceful pleasure to be had
Looking out - across the view ahead.

Two small rivers, Box and Brett
Meet the Stour at Higham.
And thus combined they softly roll
Through Dedham - to this estuary.

These lands were formed by ice and flood
By rising seas and constant flows
To lay the contours of the hills
And plot the river's certain course.

This land, this river, both unchanged
From ages past until today.
I know that I'm just passing through
Privileged to linger here.

My life will leave no lasting mark
Upon these perfect ancient lands.
The tides of life will ebb and flow
And wash all trace of me away.

+ + +

Jack And Jill

Jack and Jill
Went up the hill
To fetch a pail of water
Jack said "Please"
Jill said "Yes"
And did what she didn't ought 'a

(with acknowledgements)

+ + +

A Tribute To Anthony

Dear Belinda.
It was with a shock
And great sadness
That I read -
Of Anthony's death
In the paper
At the weekend.

And I would like to offer
My condolences
To you
And the whole family.

Anthony really was
The kindest
And most sympathetic
Of people.

And I remember fondly
The generous hospitality
That he
You
And your wonderful children
Showed to me -
When I was based
With the Army
At Topcliffe -
All those years ago.

The opportunity
To visit you all
At Barningham
Provided the most wonderful moments
Of peace and tranquillity
In a rather stressful
And hectic
Military life.

And I will be
Forever
Grateful to you all.

I remember
The horse show -
And the privilege
Of helping Anthony
Construct the jumps
For the cross country course
Through the woods.

I recall the pleasure
Of walking
- With Anthony
Across
The most beautiful of moors.

Or sitting and chatting
With him,
Whisky in hand
Late into the evening.

I will never forget
The pride
And honour I felt
When driving Alexina
To school.
In my little green VW Beetle.
On my way back
To barracks
After staying overnight
With you all.

Above everything,
I remember the warmth,
Friendship and hospitality
Of the wonderful life
Which you and he
Made with your whole family
At Barningham.

So this letter of sadness
To mark Anthony's passing,
Is also one
Of gratitude.

That I once had the joy
Of knowing him
And of sharing
Some precious time.
With him,
With you
And with Alexina, Edward and Toby:
Your whole wonderful family.

And it is that warm family
Which will enable you
To face the future,
For which you have
My very best wishes.

+ + +

Embers

Was there really any point to it all?
What useful purpose have I served
While living out my bleak and lonely life?

Searching for answers, many men
Gaze into the dying embers of a fire
And measure their life's worth therein.
So too have I been gazing –
Into the dying embers of my life
And taking the measure of my worth.

There will be no statue to celebrate my life.
No awards to mark some great achievement.
No learnèd books to argue and explain
A great contribution made to help mankind.

Like an early evening shadow, dancing
Across the choppy waters of the bay,
I too have crept silently through life
Un-noticed, un-seen and un-remarked.

And just as that shadow will vanish
Un-remembered with the setting sun,
So too will my life fade from view
And leave no passing mark upon the earth.

+ + +

Did I Mention The View?

The view.
The banter.
The pint of cold beer.
And children
Running carefree.

The view.
The game.
The murmur
Of traffic
On the road.
The church in the distance.

The wives and girlfriends
Off to the left.
With their barbeque
And children
And cold
Bottles of wine.

Did I mention the view?

Bob wanders up
With his neighbour's dog.
And Pete saunters over
To join in the chat.

Out to the front
On the field of play
The thirteen men
Continue their game.

Did I mention the view?

Leather on willow
And sometimes a call
From the players in white
Howzat?
For a catch.

But lift up your eyes
And look all around
At the trees
And the bushes
That frame this ground.

Did I mention the view?

Let no-one tell you
That green is just green.
There are so many shades
Scattered around.

The trees in the distance.
Or those
Right up close.

The newly trimmed hedge
Flat on the top.
The green of the outfield.
And the green of the square.

Greens that are dark
And some that are light.
With tinges of yellow.
Or some flecked with brown.

This is the MCC.
That's Mistley
Cricket Club.

Did I mention the view?
It's superb!

+ + +

A Little Shop In Manningtree

There's a little shop in Manningtree
Number 28 above the door
Non-descript outside
But a treasure trove within.

This little store a metaphor
For the journey we call "Life"
The window display brightly lit
Filled with tempting *bric-a-brac.*

Looking from the outside
All is dark within
So impossible to see
The goods arranged for sale.

Step across the threshold
Boldly or with fear
You may find what you're looking for
Or you may just be surprised.

Entering the store called "Life"
We will never know
What it is we'll find within
Or what – indeed – finds us.

+ + +

The Old Man

The room is small and sparsely furnished
One lone picture hanging on the wall.
Along one side a narrow bed
Takes the whole of that wall and lurks
Beneath a torn and tatty bedspread.

A basic table sits between the bed
And a simple wooden wardrobe.
On the left a four-drawer chest
Huddles beneath a metal framed window
That struggles to keep the winter storm outside.

In the middle of the floor, taking all the space
An upright chair - of utility not comfort -
Within which an old man sits in quiet dignity.
Wearing black tee-shirt under striped pyjamas
Wrapped around with shabby dressing gown
That has seen many better days.

The man, it's clear, was once quite tall
But now with shoulders slumped
And nothing on his frame
He looks broken, beaten down by age
And by life's cruel circumstance.

Above the tops of mis-matched socks
In the gap below pyjama legs
Brittle white shins with skin like paper
Give a hint to his true age.
Wispy stubble dances on a face that has seen no razor
These last ten or fifteen days.

His rheumy eyes look straight ahead
Into the far distance and beyond the room.
Not through blindness but because his mind
Replays the visions of his life
While trying not to see
This little box wherein he spends his days.

His fingers, long and bony, form grasping hands
That fold across and round a loose-leaf binder
That he holds tightly to his chest.
Despite the fertile mind that spurred him on
This file with modest poems inside
- What he used to call "his scribblings" -
Is all that's left to mark his time on earth.

His hair, though full of growth is snowy white
Which means he has just days to live.
For the men of his family line,
As they each approach the end
Of their allotted time on earth,
Lose all colour in their hair
And it turns to purest white
Five days before they lose their life.

You may look but will not see
The loneliness he's carried all his life.
No friends have come to call and wish him well
Or ask about his health.
Wherever he went he made acquaintances
With ease and with much mutual pleasure
But as he went through life's long journey
Deep friendships seemed to pass him by.

For he built walls to keep the world out
And those high boundaries kept him in.
And few it was who reached across
And tried to hold him close.
So when he had a tale to tell
Of all that he had seen and done
There were none to listen,
None to share his joy.

His mind is damaged now and has been so
For many years long passed.
But when the stress and panics clear
To give him some respite,
He sees his past with clarity
And replays it like a film within his mind.

The early years on Exmoor in the rolling hills
Gave the love of open space which never left his heart.
Then to rural Dorset and that Jurassic coast
Before the deserts of Arabia opened up a whole new world.
He's swam in the Pacific and also in the Nile
And stood on the edge of the Rift Valley
To marvel at the view.

He's walked across the mountain border
Into Turkey from Iran
Under Mount Ararat's watchful ancient gaze.
And stood on the banks of the Dnipro River
Looking east across the Russian vastness.

In his later life he still loved the open spaces.
The rolling hills of Suffolk and the valley of the Stour
Set the boundaries of his life
But he was happy there.

Now he knew his life had reached its end.
Enclosed within this tiny room
He knew that there was no way out.
No more distant views to see
No return once more to sites he'd loved.
But he could still see them in his mind.

And just as that old man can clearly see
All his life that's gone before
I can see the future too
And that old man is me.

+ + +

Manningtree Quay

Standing on the quay
At Manningtree
Looking out across
The sun-bright scene.

A haze of mist rises
Far ahead
And casts a natural veil
Over the Suffolk hills.

The river Stour is tidal here
So ebbs and flows
With every wax and waning
Of the passing moon.

Now the tide is out.
The broad and gentle river
Just a narrow channel
Through the estuary.

Boats rest gently
On the banks of mud
Waiting for the tide
To lift them clear.

Wading birds
By many thousands
Forage
As they peck and scrape.

River weed
Bright and gleaming green
Drinks in sunlight
From the crystal air.

On the right
A line of trees
Shows the road
To Mistley.

At my back
The smallest town
Goes about
Its bustling business.

To the left
Is Dedham Vale
And Flatford
Sketched by Constable.

The natural beauty
Of this land
Well known for ages
Long gone by.

Just seven years
I've lived here now
Years of peace
And friendship.

As if the very land
Itself
Had wrapped me
In its warm embrace.

And when the stress
And panics came
Said to me
"Take comfort here".

+ + +

I am on a campaign to change where we put
the question mark [?] in the English language

?Where Should The Question Mark Go

There's a flaw in the English language
I decided long ago
And that's the simple question
Of where the question mark should go.

They said you'll know it's a question
If it starts with a question word
The who, what, why and when –
But I said that's just absurd.

For every who and what and why
Designed to start a question
When sometimes used but not to ask
It only makes a statement.

When will you join me? I might ask
When I've finished what I'm doing.
What are you working on right now?
What is on the table.

Who will know that piece of work?
Who next comes to read it.
Why take note of what you say?
Why water flows downhill.

Avoid confusion: join my plan
And move the question mark.
?Don't you think it makes more sense
To put it at the start.

Before you even take your breath
Or start to say a sentence
You know a question looms ahead.
?What could then be clearer.

+ + +

Finding My Voice

Dark outside, the wind blew strong
The rain was hard and icy -
I went to call upon my friend
And share some idle chatter.

This time, my turn to take the drinks
The *Sekt* was chilled and welcome -
And eating olives, green and black
We cursed the world around us.

I'd scribbled since the last we met
Now keen to share my writing -
I took the poems I had made
And searched for something new.

A few he hadn't heard before
So listened as I read them -
The careful words came tumbling out
My soul laid bare before him.

"You've really found your voice"
He said, with kindly praise -
"That's fine" I said, still hesitant
"But has my voice found me?".

+ + +

No One Knew

No one knew just what I did
Or what I'd heard
Or what I'd seen.
No one knew just where I'd lived
Or where I'd walked
Or where I'd been.

No one knew my real name
My family's past
Or where was home.
No one knew the thoughts I'd had
The dreams I'd dreamt
Or where I'd roam.

No one knew the weight I bore
The family name
The burden carried.
No one knew the stress I felt
The angry demons
I had parried.

No one knew the walls I built
That kept them out
But kept me blind.
No one knew the pain I felt
As bit by bit
I lost my mind.

+ + +

The Tales Of Youth

On Christmas Eve I go up to bed
And I have a little cry:
Sixty-five years of loneliness
And I have to wonder why.

'Tis the season to be jolly
- Or so that we are told -
But here and now I feel no joy
Now that I grow old.

Looking back, I think once more
Of those I used to know
- Or of those I used to love
A love I could not show.

The emptiness a deeper pit
And harder still to bear
The tales of youth ring hollow now
And harder now to share.

+ + +

Sacred Sanctuary

Leave the noisy world behind
Walk boldly through the door.
Leave the stress of modern life
And step
Across the threshold.

Feel the air change as you enter -
Cooler now
Without the sun's oppressive heat.

Feel the history of this ancient place
A sanctuary for many years.

Look around in awe
- And gaze in wonder -
At the structure that enfolds you.

As your eyes accustom to the gloom
See the colours that surround you.
See the shaft of golden sunbeam
Streaming in from up on high,
Falling like a burst of holy light
Upon some religious statuary.

Look up and trace the columns as they rise
Straight as pillars first they climb.
Then arch to form the roof - high overhead -
Scattered with pin-pricks of light
Like stars across an evening sky.

A sense of calm and full of faith
Sacred as any holy site
This no dry and dusty mausoleum
But full of life and calming for the soul.

No architect designed these buttressed walls
Or carved the windows up on high.
No thatcher interlaced the roof
Giving shelter far below.
No painter came with brush in hand
To scatter his palette all around
And colour in this sacred scene.

Rather this is nature's work:
Foundations laid down long ago
From which have grown the noble trees
Of this ancient wood wherein you stand.

+ + +

In My Old Age

In my old age
I'm feeling my age.
I know I'm getting old -
Because I get up several times in the night.

Sometimes I make a cup of tea
And sometimes I don't.
But always I go to the loo.

I have a friendly spider
Living in my bathroom.
That only comes out at night.
In the dark.

When I put the light on it gets confused
So I always apologise.
For disturbing his night.
Which is really his working day.

We're now close friends
And I check that he's there.
Which he always is.

He's got a new friend
So now there are two.
Similar spiders
checking their web - together.

The other night I heard them.
Chatting -
One to another.
While I did my business.

And one of them said
One to the other:
When I get old
I honestly hope
That in my old age
I really don't need
To go to the loo every night.

+ + +

Keep It Simple

Few there are
Who coast along
Or glide their
Way through life.

Pushed and pulled
By winds and tides
Of everyday existence
We struggle as we seek –
To lead our fragile lives
Of quiet desperation

Fears of health
Of debt or work
Constantly intrude
And raise the question
?What's it for
This challenge
That is life.

Keep it simple
Do not strive
Or seek to over-do.
Set modest goals
That you can reach
And by that reaching
Triumph!

Contentment and a peaceful life
Will come to those who know
A modest target that is met
Beats a higher one
That's missed

+ + +

The Ebbing Tide

Sitting on the river bank
Taking in this peaceful scene
Gazing out across the flat
Clear, waters of the estuary.

Looking north to rolling Suffolk.
Patchwork fields of green
Growing brighter in the sun
As spring grows daily stronger.

A dozen snow-white swans
Gliding east in line astern
Dwarf the wading birds
Grubbing at the water's edge.

Boats out on the water
Swing gently with the tide
And point their bows upstream
To Flatford and to Dedham.

That tide is past its high –
And ebbing now it rushes
Eastward in a headlong race
To catch the open sea.

So it seems is my life:
Now well past the high
Ebbing too, it surely drains
Towards its certain end.

And just as these waters
Grew and gathered strength
As they flowed ever on
Towards the open sea

So it was with my life:
Building on the scenes I saw
And places that I went
That brought me to this spot

Where I can sit in peace
At one with this wide river
As - side by side - we drift
Towards our natural end.

+ + +

The Forgotten Man

It starts with just the little things
Such as not remembering a name.
He looked vaguely familiar and smiled
- As I passed him in the street.

He called a cheery greeting
And addressed me by my name.
I smiled back out of courtesy
- And mumbled as we passed.

I knew I ought to know him
But my brain had let me down.
So I've spent the whole time since
In wondering who he was.

+ + +

Dreaming

In the springtime of my life
I started dreaming.
I dreamed of where I'd go
And what I'd do.
I dreamed of what I'd see
And what I'd build.
I dreamed of breaking free
- And setting out -
Upon my chosen path.

As the years went by
I fell behind
The pattern of my dreams.
But still they spurred me on
And I dared to keep on dreaming.
Even then I knew
That all men must have dreams
- For without them -
What is there to aim for.

Now in the autumn of my life
I dream again.
But these are different dreams:
Not dreams of the future
- Plans to drive me on -
But jumbled, muddled dreams
Of the distant past.

Dreams of what I'd seen
And what I'd heard.
Dreams of where I'd walked
And what I'd done,
As, bit by bit, my troubled mind
Seeks to make some sense
- Of all that's gone before -
And made me who I am.

+ + +

Burning Paper

It matters not the time of day
Morning, noon or night
No warning call is given out,
- It suddenly appears.

Just at first a little sniff
Announces its arrival
Then pungent, deep and stinging,
- Soon it's over-powering.

The smell of burning paper
Acrid, sharp and thick
Gets in to the nostrils
- And fills the brain with fear.

Sometimes just a fleeting smell
Quickly come and gone
Recognised for what it is:
- A figment of the mind.

Other times it lingers more
Playing with the senses
Filling up the eyes with tears,
- Bitter on the tongue.

There is no burning paper
No reason for the dread,
Just the frenzied workings
- Of a damaged temporal lobe.

+ + +

These Ancient Lands

I walked along the river's edge
With Mistley at my back
The rising sun behind me
Lit up the land ahead

As it climbed it cast its spell
Across these ancient lands
Turned the cold grey light of dawn
To colour and to clarity

Distant woods that once were cast
In dull and sombre tones
Appearing now both proud and tall
In colours deep and bold

The land itself a patchwork
Of yellows, browns and greens
Shaking off the dark of night
To face the bright new day

From ages past these lands have shaped
The people who have lived here
The farmers and the artisans
And those who worked the sea

Man arrogantly seems to think
It's he who forms the land
But look a bit more closely
And you'll see the land shapes him

Cut and carved by fire and ice
Through aeons now long past
Nature's work continues on
- The land is never finished.

+ + +

In A Panic

A friend rang in a panic
I've got a mole she cried in despair.
Calm down I said take it easy
There's no point in making a fuss.
They're not such a problem I told her
An expert will soon sort you out
Your mole will be gone in a jiffy
You needn't be making a scene.

It's not just the one
She screamed down the phone
There's lots I can suddenly see
And I'm sure there are many
That haven't appeared yet
But will come in to view any day.

It's quite normal I told her
At your time of life
To suddenly find you've got moles.
An expert will help you
They'll know what to do
And your problem will soon be gone.
Just treat them with care
Don't pick them or scratch them
You don't know what's underneath.

But my insurance has lapsed
And I don't have much money
She continued to cry in a wail.
Just calm down I said
And do what I say
The sooner to start on a fix.
If you linger they'll spread
And take longer to cure
So book an appointment right now.

Well you're not much good
She cried in disgust
I thought you'd be able to help.
I need something done
Right now if not sooner
These moles will ruin my lawn.

+ + +

The Talented Mr D.

A friend of mine makes films
He makes very good films.
They always get great reviews
Although they're difficult to make.

It's hard to raise the money
and it's hard to find the cast
And put it all together
To get it in the can.

But the work doesn't stop
When the film is released.
As it has to be sold
To get the film seen.
On the screen.

So off he goes
Around the world.
A film festival here
Or an opening night there.
Somewhere quite local
Or across the globe.
All with the aim
Of plugging his film.
And it can be a drag!

And one balmy night,
After the showing
Of The Deep Blue Sea.
At the electric cinema
In Harwich
Of all places
Just up the road
A lady got up with a question:
Could you tell me
She said
With an air of disdain
Why in your film
Not once did you mention The Queen.

Well
Said my friend
I believe it's quite true
That when The Queen makes a film
She doesn't mention me.

+ + +

Life's Corridor

Walking down life's corridor
I stroll past many doors –
Some I notice, some I don't
And very few I open.

On some I turn the handle
But never look inside –
Some sixth sense has spoken:
That room is not for me.

Some rooms that I enter
Having opened wide the door –
Provide a feast of what I need
At that point in my life.

Some rooms turned out not to give
What I was hoping for –
But even here they added to
The journey of my life.

Now I've turned a corner
Rooms are getting scarce –
Not so many doors to open
Giving me less choice.

Now more rooms behind me
Than there are in front –
The end of life's rich corridor
Is looming up ahead.

The paint on walls is peeling
The doors are all locked shut –
The carpet, stained and threadbare
A growing sense of gloom.

The longer that I tread this path
More time I have to think –
Of what was in those many rooms
I entered long ago.

I Didn't Die Last Night

I didn't die last night.
I don't know why.
But much to my surprise
I didn't die last night.

I didn't die last night
Though I thought I would.
I really did expect it.
But I didn't die last night.

It just never happened
Despite the night I had
- With very little sleep.
But I didn't die last night.

My head was in a turmoil
All tangled in a mess
- Ready to explode.
But I didn't die last night.

Getting up at dawn
I felt all disconnected
My head was out of kilter.
But I didn't die last night.

Going for a morning walk
Along the river bank
I really couldn't understand
How I didn't die last night.

The air was crystal clear
The sky so bright and blue
The scene itself bought calm
To my tortured head.

Living with such beauty
Fills my heart with joy.
So I'm very glad to say
That I didn't die last night.

+ + +

Death Came Rushing

Death came rushing down the street
I saw her getting closer
I pressed against the nearby wall
And hoped she hadn't seen me.

She opened wide her grasping arms
To make her cold embrace
And fixed me with her mocking stare
Thinking that she's got me.

I didn't want to die just then
I really wasn't ready
Still too many things to do
And places yet to visit.

As I ducked and twisted free
She grabbed at empty air.
This time I had cheated her
And lived to tell the tale.

+ + +

A Sophisticated Lady

She's a sophisticated lady
With sophisticated airs.
She has a hint of haughtiness
Putting others in their place.

She's not *quite* as well educated
As she likes to think she is.
But Daddy's fees weren't wasted
As she learnt her place in life.

She's not *quite* as beautiful
As she's always been assured.
She doesn't have an accent
But speaks in best RP.

She seems to be well travelled
But there's *travelling* and *travelling*.
Never in Economy
Always up in First.

She'll greet you hale and hearty
While looking down her nose.
She doesn't do sincerity
And never slips the mask.

?How best to sum her up
By using just a phrase.
It may sound cruel to say it –

But she spells phuck with a PH.

+ + +

Looking Back With Love

When you're getting old
And in the autumn of your life,
Sitting in your favourite chair
And wrapped against the cold,
Let slip the chains that hold your mind
And set it loose to run –
Back again to sunny days
When you were in your prime.

Replay once more within your mind
Those days of light and love –
Watch again those happy scenes
Of warmer times long gone.
And play them, like a film,
Across the theatre of your mind
Fresh and crisp, to you now,
As the day you lived them.

Close your eyes and see once more
So clearly in your mind
That young man you used to know
And loved so much it hurt.
In your mind you raise your hand
And reach towards my head
And touch again my laughing face
And look in to my eyes.

Now many years since last we met
And held me to your heart
But no amount of time can wipe
The memories you hold.
You see me as I used to be
And in your mind you still
Picture me as I once was
And to you have stayed.

+ + +

60

Blowing Eggs

In the springtime of my years
We lived a rural life.
Fields to run through
Trees to climb
And hedges to explore.

My parents had
A herd of goats
At the foot of Bulbarrow Hill.
Grass for the goats
Fresh milk for us
Who could ask for more?

The patterns and the seasons
Of a natural, country life
Went on all around us
In a rhythm
Still unchanging
From many years long gone.

We sought out nesting birds
And took for our collection
Just one egg.
And piercing with a pin
At each end
We blew the innards out.

What was left was just a shell.
Attractive, yes
And colourful.
But hiding that
Within was nothing
But just emptiness.

And so, as I take stock
Of the balance of my life
I get once more to thinking
How the circle has now turned.
No longer young and agile
As I used to be.

And looking from the outside
My life appears to be
Just like those eggs
I used to blow.
Attractive, yes
And colourful.

But hiding that
Within is nothing
– But just emptiness.

+ + +

Deo Gratias

I loved you once.

Though I say 'once'
That 'once' continued on
For five and thirty years.

When I was aged
But just eighteen
You took me to your life
Until, when I was fifty-three
You lost your mind.

And then, by that losing
I in turn lost mine
Which, to this day
- Just like my heart –
Has never mended.

+ + +

The Greenest Grass

Just how tall
Would the tall grass grow
If the tall grass grew
Real tall?

Just how green
Would the green grass grow
If the green grass grew
Real green?

Just how sweet
Would the sweet grass grow
If the sweet grass grew
Real sweet?

Just how soft
Would the soft grass grow
If the soft grass grew
Real soft?

If the grass grew
Tall and green
And the grass grew
Sweet and soft

The grass would be
The greatest gift
Given to us
By nature.

The softest grass
Could give our bed.
The sweetest grass
Our food.
The tallest grass could give
Our fuel.
Together all we need.

But the greenest grass
Gives the greatest gift
Of calm
And peace of mind.

For when the stress and strains
Of modern life
Push us to the edge
To look upon a field of green
Will calm and soothe the soul.

+ + +

Late At Night

Late at night I got to home
Returning from my travels.
You were sleeping peacefully
As I approached the bed
And lifting up the coverlet
I gently slid inside.

Wanting not to waken you
I slowly leaned across
To kiss your naked shoulder
And know once more
The heady taste –
Of your perfect skin.

In your sleep your hand reached out
And brushed against my cheek.
You knew it not but by that touch
All my chains were rent.
I broke free from the bonds of earth
And flew among the stars.

+ + +

Longing

I used to long for marriage
Either in law or just in fact.
To have such a close relationship
With just one other human being
Would have made me whole.

I thought that I had found it
The three times I was engaged
Thinking I had found my soulmate.
But each was spoilt by late discovery
And none was meant to be.

Every time I hear the strain
Of Mendelssohn's wedding march
I break a little bit inside
Knowing that I will never stand
While a bride approaches to that tune.

As I wait to say "I do".

+ + +

Welcome to Winter

It's colder now.
The changing of the clocks brought a change of weather too.
With cold winds blowing from the north and cutting to the
bone.

This year autumn lingered.
With unexpected tricks of light to flatter and confuse.
Clear bright air and days of warmth to tease us and enthral.

Trees are quickly changing.
Their bright and vivid summer greens are dull and laced with
dust.
Yellow and red the colours now of leaves that haven't fallen.

The tide is high but turning.
The water here is rough, no longer smooth and flat.
White horses play and dance about, whipped up by the wind.

Boats out on the river.
Tossed by unforgiving squalls they fight to hold their station.
And all as one they keep their bows heading 'gainst the tide.

Clouds low overhead.
No longer light and slowly drifting, across the clear-blue sky.
But heavy, grey and threatening, full of darkened menace.

The light has changed.
No longer crystal clear and full of airy sparkle -
But tinged with blue and hinting at the coming of the cold.

Rain is now just starting.
Driven by the northern wind and feeling cold as ice -
Each individual drop of water pricking like a pin.

People hurry past.
Now not strolling by and walking slowly, taking in the view -
But striding fast and well wrapped up, protected from the
cold.

Welcome now to winter.
Much more cold and wet to come for five long months ahead.
But after that, we hope, next year the spring will come again.

+ + +

The Hearse

The hearse moved slowly
Like a shining silver wraith
Gliding through the summer scene
Along the road from Manningtree.

The coffin carried at the rear
Dressed with bunch of lilies,
Bore its dead with dignity
Upon their final journey.

Following the river's edge
Alongside green and grassy verge
Over-hung with agèd trees
Seeing all from up on high.

The tidal river full and flat
Gleaming in the summer sun
Boats at anchor, lying still
Upon the peaceful estuary.

On the northern Suffolk shore
Hedges dressed in dusty green
Mark boundaries of ancient fields
Like patchwork on the land.

Carefree people strolling by
Taking in this tranquil scene
Noticed not the hearse go by
Nor wondered who it carried.

From anywhere along this road
Looking out across the water,
In any season, any month
This sight will lift the soul.

I know these views from living here
Few there are much better
But passing now I see them not
While lying in my coffin.

+ + +

Missing The Boat

"You've missed the boat"
They shouted
As I ran along the quay.

The engines roared
It picked up speed
And left me far behind.

+ + +

When I Die

When I die, mourn not my passing
But celebrate my life.
If you knew me, then I knew you too,
And you touched my life
– As I touched yours.

Throw a stone into a pond
And ripples spread in ever widening circles.
So the ripples of my life spread
– To touch the lives of many others.

But in my turn I was touched
– By the many ripples of your lives –
And for that I thank you all.
For you have helped to shape my life
And make me who I am.

Truly as a spring tide rises highest,
So have your ripples
– Joining together –
Made a spring tide for my life:
Lifting me higher
Than I could have ever reached
– If I had never known you.

+ + +

Index of First Lines

Printed in Great Britain
by Amazon